Discover other cultures

Puppets
Around The World

Meryl Doney

About this book

In this book you will find examples of puppets from a wide variety of countries and backgrounds. The puppet theatre of each country has its own distinctive style, with different designs, colours and traditions. When you have decided which puppets you would like to make, begin by looking at the relevant maps to see where the puppets come from.

Try to find other books on the particular countries and their culture, and read all about them. When you come to decorate your puppets, the theatre and props, use traditional designs or patterns copied from these reference books. This will help to make your puppet theatre more like the real thing.

Adapt the ideas from this book freely as you go along, and invent your own puppet characters.

Most of the steps are very easy to follow, but where you see this sign ask for help from an adult.

Performing plays

Many puppet performances around the world take place in the open air, with a minimum amount of equipment. This makes the puppets very easy to use. On pages 28–29 you will find some notes on staging plays in this way, with instructions for building three simple stages. There is also a play idea in which all the puppets in this book can appear.

When you have made your characters, you may prefer to develop a traditional play for them to perform. Such plays are usually drawn from the history of a particular country, from traditional fables, religious stories or moral tales. Your local library will have a good collection of stories from around the world, and you can simplify and adapt them to suit the puppets you have made.

Originally published as World Crafts: Puppets

This edition first published in 2002
© Franklin Watts 1995, 2002
Text © Meryl Doney 1995

Franklin Watts
96 Leonard Street, London EC2A 4XD

Franklin Watts Australia
56 O'Riordan Street, Alexandria, NSW 2015

ISBN: 0 7496 4548 2 (pbk)
Dewey Decimal Classification Number 745.592

Series editor: Annabel Martin
Editor: Jane Walker
Design: Visual Image
Cover design: Chloë Cheesman/Mike Davis
Artwork: Ruth Levy
Photography: Peter Millard

With special thanks to Alison Croft, educational advisor and puppet maker

A CIP catalogue record for this book is available from the British Library

Printed in Dubai

Contents

Puppet history

Traditional puppet theatres exist in almost every country in the world. One of the earliest puppets, a monkey character, was discovered in India and may be over 4,000 years old. There are also early records of plays about legendary heroes and gods being acted by shadow, rod and marionette puppets in China and the Far East.

From these early beginnings in Asia, entertainers and their puppets probably travelled along the great trading routes. As the entertainers moved from place to place they would stop and perform for the local people. In this way they spread the art of puppetry across the ancient world.

The Greeks and Romans included puppets in their religious plays, and the first Christians used them to teach Bible stories. When the Roman Empire fell apart, actors and puppeteers again travelled across Europe entertaining everyone from kings to the crowds in the market-place. The Italian clown, Pulcinello, grew out of this tradition, and from him the Mr Punch glove puppet evolved.

Puppets were brought to North America and Australia in the nineteenth century by emigrants from Europe. There is some evidence, however, that the North American Indians and Aboriginal peoples of Australia had their own puppet tradition before then.

Today, puppets are more popular than ever. Many famous characters have been created for international TV programmes such as *Sesame Street* and *The Muppet Show*, as well as for feature films.

We hope you enjoy making your puppets and giving pleasure to others as you perform your own plays.

Your own puppet-making kit

As you begin making your puppets, look around for odd bits of material, buttons, cardboard tubes and yoghurt pots. Keep these items in a box with a set of tools ready for when you want to make a puppet.

Make some dough from the recipes below and store that too. Wrap it in cling film and keep it in a container with a tight lid.

Here are some of the most useful items for your puppet-making kit:

hammer • tenon saw • hacksaw • awl • hand drill • needle-nosed pliers • scissors • craft knife • staple gun • metal ruler • brushes • white emulsion • poster paints • varnish • PVA (white) glue • tube of strong glue • plastic modelling material • modelling clay • sticky tape • masking tape • card •

paper • tissue paper • newspaper • pen • pencil • felt pens • fabric and felt • needle and thread • decorations, including sequins, braid, tin foil, sticky shapes, beads • newspaper to work on • card to cut on • apron • paper towels for cleaning up

Potato dough

This dough recipe comes from Peru. It is made from mashed potatoes and plaster of Paris.

3 tablespoons of instant mashed potato
10 tablespoons of plaster of Paris
water

In a small bowl, mix up the mashed potato with 150 ml of boiling water. Beat with a fork until floury.

In a larger bowl, mix the plaster with 3 tablespoons of cold water. Stir with a spoon until smooth.

Add the potato to the plaster and mix well. Form into a dough and knead well.

No cooking is required for this dough.

Salt dough

2 cups of flour
1/2 cup of salt
3/4 cup of water

Mix the flour and salt together in a large bowl.

Make a well in the middle, pour in a little water and stir with a fork. Keep adding water, a little at a time, until you have used it all.

Finish mixing and kneading the dough with your hands. If it is too sticky, add more flour; if too dry, add more water.

Salt dough must be dried in the oven to produce a hard result.

Dancing puppets

These puppets, which are sometimes called jumping jacks, are very simple to make.

Here are two examples from very different settings. The little clown on the left is from Poland. He is made from sheets of tin and has a wooden head. Each side of his body is painted in different colours so that the clown can change character when he is turned around.

The Indian pop-up puppet (above) is from Calcutta, where the children make their own versions from cardboard and thread. These puppets are decorated with brightly coloured foil and sequins. This character is thought to represent Amar Singh Rathore, the hero of a traditional Rajasthan puppet play.

Make an Indian pop-up puppet

You will need: card • tin foil • glue • coloured paper • needle and thread • a garden cane • sticky tape • decorations

1 Cut simple body parts from card. Glue on pieces of foil and coloured paper to form face and uniform. Cover shield and sabre with tin foil. Make two small holes in the top of each arm and leg. Make four holes in the body as shown.

2 Join arms together with thread. Use the holes that are nearest the edges. Knot at the back. Join legs in the same way.

3 Attach arms to body with thread, using the bottom holes on arms. Knot at the back and front. Attach legs in the same way.

4 Use another thread to join the arms and legs, so that you can make the puppet jump.

Cover the back by glueing a piece of coloured paper onto the back of the neck.

5 Split the top 2 cm of a small, green garden cane. Push puppet into it and secure with tape. Neaten split end and knots by covering with tin foil. Attach shield and sabre.

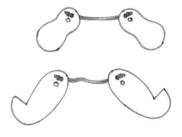

Hand puppets

China has a history of puppet-making which goes back over 2,000 years. This glove puppet is based on the historic Ku Li Tzu puppet theatre. The puppeteer carried his puppets from town to town in a small box-like theatre slung from the end of a pole. To begin the show, he would prop the pole against a wall and unroll curtains from below the stage to hide himself. After the show he would hoist the whole thing onto his shoulder again and move on to the next village.

Like the characters in Chinese opera, this puppet's face is painted to show his personality. He is a young man because he has no beard. You could make your puppet angry or sad, young or old, depending on the story you plan to perform. You may be able to find designs for faces in a book on Chinese opera.

Make a Ku Li Tzu puppet

You will need: salt dough (see recipe, page 5) · a cork · paints · varnish · card · PVA glue · coloured fabric · white or beige fabric · ribbon · felt pen · rice (uncooked)

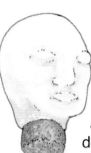

1 To make the head, take a piece of dough about the size of a ping pong ball. Push a cork into it and mould more dough around the cork to form the neck. Model the chin and add small pieces of dough for the facial features.

2 For boots, roll two small sausage shapes. Bend into L-shapes, flatten soles and point toes. Model two smaller pieces of dough into hands. Bake all dough shapes at 150°C (gas mark 2) until hard (about 40 minutes). Remove cork and leave head to cool in oven.

3 Paint all the pieces white, then add colour and varnish.

4 Cut out four pieces from card for the head-dress. Glue rectangle around head, fold in sides and staple at top. Glue on other pieces of card and decorate.

front

back

5 Cut out fabric pieces for the robe. Pin and sew them, right sides together, leaving arm and neck holes. Hem. Decorate with felt pen. Glue head and hands into the holes and turn robe the right side out. Trim the neck with ribbon.

Sewing hint: If you sew one way with running stitch, and then come back again filling in the spaces, you will make a strong seam.

6 Cut out front panel and hem it. Decorate with felt pen. Sew to front of robe. Make legs from two rectangles of white fabric. Sew up the sides to make tubes. Turn right side out and glue a boot into each tube. Fill legs with rice, leaving 4 cm empty at top.

7 Fold in 1 cm of fabric and pin legs inside front of robe under panel. Sew.

Papier mâché glove puppets

Mr Punch, as we know him today, is a puppet with a fascinating history. As far as we can discover, he began life in Italy as a funny character called Pulcinello. Italian puppets were based on a popular drama known as the *commedia dell'arte*, in which there were several clowns, or *zanni*, to keep the people laughing. Pulcinello was a little man with a very hooked nose and chin, and a hunched back. He wore a ruff round his neck and had a pointed hat with a bell.

Mr Punch was brought to England in about 1660, and he soon became a popular character. At that time he was a marionette, not a glove puppet. Everyone loved the puppet plays because the puppeteers used them to poke fun at the authorities. By 1825 Mr Punch had a wife, Joan (her name later changed to Judy), and the puppet stories had become firm favourites.

Make Mr Punch

Traditional Punch characters were carved from wood, but this one has a papier mâché head and a fabric body. The head is quite big compared to the body, but it must be light so that your hand can move the puppet easily.

To perform a traditional play you will also need to make Judy, her baby, the policeman and the crocodile.

You will need: newspaper • piece of firm card • masking tape • light card • PVA glue • toothpick • plastic modelling material • cotton wool • paints • varnish • cotton fabric • felt • ric rac braid • a bell

1 Scrunch paper into a head shape and stick it onto card with masking tape. Roll a piece of card round your finger and tape it to make a tube. Push tube under the paper to form neck.

2 Push a shortened toothpick into the head so it sticks out a little. Form nose out of plastic modelling material and press onto toothpick. Add eyebrows, eyes and mouth. Add papier mâché by sticking small pieces of newspaper, in layers, over the face.

3 When dry, cut head away from card. Fill back with cotton wool. Cut out two card ears and stick to head with tape. Cover the back of head with more papier mâché and leave it to harden. Paint with white emulsion before painting features with coloured paints. Varnish.

4 To dress Mr Punch, cut out two fabric bodies. Pin and sew, leaving the neck and bottom edge open. Turn the right way out and neaten hem. Sew a running stitch along the edge of a strip of felt to make a drawstring for the ruff.

5 Measure halfway around head and make a pattern for hat. Cut from felt, and sew. Cut a separate piece for brim. Cut out four hand shapes. Decorate clothes with ric rac braid.

6 Glue neck of body to head tube and tie on ruff with drawstring. Glue hat and brim to head. Glue hands together, leaving cuffs open. Glue hands to his arms. Add a bell to his hat!

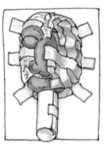

Carved wooden puppets

These African figures seem at first sight to be very different from many people's idea of puppets. They have few moving parts and are more like carved figures or masks. However, they are genuine puppets, which are used by storytellers to teach history, to tell legendary tales and to pass on the values of the tribe or village group.

The woman puppet on the left is a Marka marionette from Tenne in Mali. The Marka, who are part of the Senoufo tribe, use these puppets to tell traditional fables. She is carved from one piece of wood, and her face and head are decorated with strips of tin nailed to the surface. Her arms are operated by pulling a string from below.

The warrior on the right, with his shield and scimitar, is from Tunisia, North Africa. He may be the same character as the Indian dancing puppet, Amar Singh Rathore, on page 6. If so, he has travelled to North Africa from India. Puppet characters often moved from country to country as entertainers travelled on the trade routes.

The warrior is a puppet with no strings. The storyteller would probably hold him in his hand and act out the story for his audience.

Make an African warrior

1 Mark out the puppet's features on the large piece of wood, using one corner as his nose. Grip in a vice and use a craft knife to cut out the features.

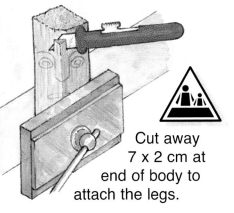

Cut away 7 x 2 cm at end of body to attach the legs.

2 Cut a 5-cm piece off the end of each leg and glue it on at right angles, to form feet. Cut a piece 1 x 6 cm from top of each leg. Use craft knife to cut out wrist shape at one end of each hand. Cut V shapes for fingers. Paint all pieces white before decorating with poster paint. Varnish.

3 Use a knitting needle to make holes through the legs and body. Thread a piece of wire through the leg, washer, body, washer and leg. Twist the ends so that the legs are secure but move freely.

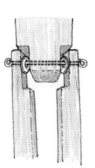

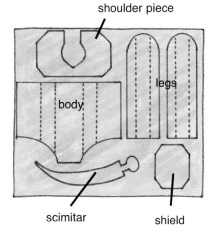

shoulder piece

legs

body

scimitar

shield

4 Draw all the pieces of armour on gold card. Cut out and decorate by scoring and denting with a blunt pencil.

5 Sew the sides of skirt together and hem. Sew a running stitch around top and pull to gather. Sew down one side of each arm piece, turn right side out and iron flat. Staple hands to arms.

6 Staple dress to waist and arms to shoulders. Wrap armour around body, add shoulder piece and staple to back. Staple armour pieces to legs, shield to one hand and scimitar to the other.

Shadow puppets

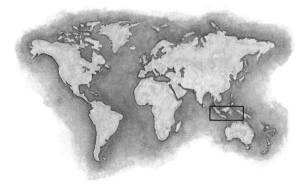

The fascinating art of the shadow puppet may have begun in South-East Asia, and there is still a strong tradition of these puppets in Indonesia, China and India.

Originally shadow puppets represented people's ancestors, whose spirits were invited to enter the puppets. The spirits gave messages and advice on family matters or in times of danger. Today the plays are mostly seen as entertainments or ways of teaching people, but there is still something magical about the performances.

In a typical shadow theatre the puppets are held against a white screen, which is tightly stretched across a wooden frame.

The performance begins in the evening, lit from behind by an oil lamp, and can go on all night. The puppet master has to be a man of many talents. He operates the puppets, tells the story, directs the orchestra and sometimes even plays a musical instrument as well!

This is a Wayang Kulit puppet from Java in Indonesia. The word *wayang* means 'shadow', and *kulit* means 'skin' or 'leather'.

Make a Wayang Kulit puppet

You will need: cereal box card • gold poster paint • paints • varnish • a needle • plastic modelling material • split pins/brass fasteners • 3 green garden sticks

1 Draw one body and four arm pieces on card. Paint and varnish your design.

3 Cut out the pieces. Join the arms and body together loosely with split pins. Trim the ends of the pins with scissors so that they do not stick out. Glue on garden sticks.

2 Use a needle to make a pattern of holes in the card. Place some plastic modelling material under the card as you do this. Make bigger holes at the elbows and shoulders for split pin fasteners.

To make your own shadow puppet theatre see pages 28–29.

Comic shadow puppets

Karagöz

No one knows exactly how the tradition of shadow puppets came to Europe. They may have travelled all the way from the Far East via India or Arabia. These characters from Greece and Turkey are a remarkable mixture of the *wayang* tradition of Asia (see page 14) and Mr Punch of Europe (see page 10).

Karagöz is the hero from the Turkish shadow puppet theatre. He and his friend Hacivat are rough, funny characters who enjoy lots of slapstick fun and fighting on stage. They are also very greedy and love food.

The plays are performed against a stretched screen, with an olive oil lamp providing the lighting. The colours show through the screen, making them look like stained glass. Karagöz is operated with one or two sticks, allowing him to fight, fall over and even perform a somersault with a deft twist of the puppeteer's wrist.

The stories in Greek shadow puppet theatre come from Turkey. They feature the same knockabout characters, but they are called Karagiosis and Haziavadis.

Karagiosis

Make Karagöz, the Turkish hero

Adapt this method to make other characters for your plays.

Make sure that Karagöz and Hacivat face in opposite directions so that they can talk to each other on stage.

You will need: white photocopier card • felt pens • cooking oil • plastic modelling material • split pins/brass fasteners • dowel rods, 30 cm long • drawing pins

1 Draw each puppet piece faintly on card. Colour in with felt pens. Rub cooking oil into both sides of the card to make it transparent.

3 Attach the rods to the puppet by pushing a drawing pin through the card and into the end of each dowel. To store puppets, remove rods and keep in a plastic bag, so that oil does not dry out.

2 Cut out the pieces. Make joining holes by pushing a pencil through the card into a piece of plastic modelling material. Use split pins to fix the pieces loosely together.

Hacivat

Rod puppets

Rod puppets are made from carved wooden pieces. The head is mounted on a long rod which passes through the body. The puppeteer moves the head by twisting this rod with one hand while moving the arms with two more rods held in the other hand. Rod puppets have long skirts instead of legs.

The puppet below comes from the Wayang Purwa plays, which tell traditional Hindu stories. Good and bad characters in the plays can be distinguished by the way they look. Even the angle of the puppet's head is important.

The rod puppet on the right comes from Java in Indonesia. She is a character from the famous Wayang Golek theatre, which dates back to the sixteenth century. A Moslem Javanese ruler commissioned puppeteers to help spread the Islamic religion in Java. The plays are known as the Menak Cycle.

In Wayang Golek plays the puppet master speaks all the roles, sings, narrates and works the puppets, as well as directing the *gamelan* orchestra.

Make a Menak rod puppet

You will need: two 2-cm card tubes, 15 cm and 6 cm long • light card, 5 x 8 cm • PVA glue • cardboard box, 15 x 7 x 5 cm (an empty chocolate box is ideal) • masking tape • salt dough or modelling clay • 1-cm dowel rod, 48 cm long • four 1-cm dowels, 8 cm long • paints • varnish • short fabric strips • felt • braid and beads • fabric for skirt, 45 x 50 cm • thin string • two plant sticks

1 Wrap and glue light card around the end of the longer card tube to form a cuff. Pierce each end of box, and push tube through so that it forms a central hole with cuff at top. Glue in place.

2 Squeeze box to form a body shape. Secure with masking tape. With dough or modelling clay mould a head onto the short card tube, and hands onto two short dowels. Make small holes in hands to attach sticks.

3 When dry, paint and varnish head and hands. Wrap masking tape around long dowel until it fits into head tube. Glue firmly. Attach arm pieces to each other and to the body with fabric strips. Glue in place. Make sure arms can move freely.

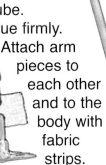

4 Cut clothes pieces from felt and decorate with braid. Sew sleeves into tube shapes. Sew jacket sides to back piece, adding in sleeves. Make a long skirt (see page 13), and tie around waist.

5 Dress puppet. Slot dowel through body so that neck rests in cuff. Tie thin string to plant sticks, thread through holes in hands and knot. Glue short strings of beads to ears.

Lifelike puppets

Japan's *bunraku* puppets, at over one metre tall, are some of the largest in the world. It takes three people to operate each puppet; one to work its head and right arm, one to work its left arm and one to work its legs. To operate the head requires the most skill, as the mouth, eyes and even the eyebrows can move. The puppeteers wear black clothes and hoods over their faces so they do not distract the audience. The puppets wear beautiful silk kimonos which are padded to form their bodies.

Many *bunraku* performances use stories which were written around 300 years ago. The puppeteers are silent, and a narrator at the side of the stage tells the story. Background music adds to the atmosphere. It is performed on the *shamisen*, a three-stringed instrument similar to a guitar. The musician, the narrator and particularly the puppeteers must work together as a team. Teamwork is highly valued in traditional Japanese culture.

Make a *bunraku* puppet

This is a simplified *bunraku* puppet which can be operated by two or three people. Our puppet does not have legs, but you could have fun working out how to make some.

You will need: a balloon • newspaper and white tissue paper • plastic modelling material • PVA glue • thick cardboard tube, 60 x 5 cm • masking tape • piece of wood for shoulders, 1.5 x 5 x 35 cm • corrugated card • paints • varnish • strong cloth, tape or ribbon, 2 x 10 cm • 2 pieces of wood for arms, 3 x 1.5 x 28 cm • 2 pieces of fabric for sleeves, 15 x 30 cm • fabric for undershirt, 25 x 40 cm • fabric for belt, 20 x 60 cm • white paper • fabric for kimono, 85 x 150 cm • 2 pieces of dowel, 60 cm long

1 Blow up and tie the balloon. 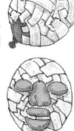 Cover with several layers of papier mâché, leaving a hole around the knot. When dry remove balloon. Mould face from plastic modelling material stuck to head. Cover with papier mâché, finishing with a layer of tissue paper.

2 Fix tube firmly in a vice and mark a point nearly in the middle. Saw a slot halfway through for wooden shoulders to fit in. Lash shoulders and tube together with masking tape.

3 Draw round your hand on corrugated card. Cut out four hands from this pattern. Glue the hands together in pairs. Paint and varnish head, neck and hands.

4 Pad shoulders with rolls of newspaper bound with masking tape. Cut two pieces of fabric tape. Staple each to shoulder and arm, allowing them to move freely. Staple hands to arms at an angle. Cover each arm with fabric glued into position.

5 Fold undershirt fabric over a rectangle of paper. Make belt in the same way.

6 Make a long T-shaped cut up the centre of the kimono fabric, 1 metre long and 18 cm across. Fold back edges and sew wide hem.

7 Put undershirt and kimono on puppet and staple to back of shoulders. Sew undershirt together at front, then the kimono. Wrap belt around and stitch at the back. Glue end of neck and push right up into head so that it sticks. Attach dowels to hands (see page 19).

21

String puppets

These puppets are the very popular Kathputli marionettes of Rajasthan in northern India. They are simple to operate as they only have one string, which runs from the top of the head to the back of the waist. Their heads and bodies are carved from one piece of mango wood, and their arms are made of stuffed cloth. Instead of legs the women have long skirts which swirl as they dance. Some of the men have skirts, and others have padded trousers which are caught at the ankle, with cloth feet.

The puppeteer gives his marionettes high-pitched voices by speaking through a bamboo and leather reed known as a *boli*.

The plays use many of the same themes as the shadow theatre. The Hindu stories *The Mahabharata* and *The Ramayana* are particularly popular. They feature supernatural beings, gods, magical monkeys and other exciting characters. The audience love to see the trick puppets such as the juggler and the horse and rider (see page 26). A special favourite is the puppet with two heads, a man's head on one side and a woman's on the other. With a deft twist the man can change into a woman and vice versa, much to the delight of the crowd.

Make a Kathputli marionette

This page shows you how to make a Kathputli puppet head by carving a piece of balsa wood. This is nearest to the method used to make these puppets in India. However, you may prefer to use another method, such as papier mâché or modelling clay.

Try making the two-headed puppet using this method. The sari for the woman should cover only half her head and hang down on one side. The man could have a different skirt or trousers on his side. The second string should be fixed on the shoulders to help you swing the puppet round and change its character.

You will need: balsa wood, 7 x 7 x 18 cm • paints • varnish • fabric for arms and head-dress, 20 x 25 cm and 5 x 7 cm • gold braid or ribbon • cotton fabric for skirt, 40 x 60 cm • small carpet tacks • two pieces of braid, 14 cm long • sari material, 62 x 38 cm • needle and two lengths of light string • braid, beads and sequins

1 Draw puppet shape on balsa wood, using one edge as the nose. Grip firmly in vice and use a craft knife to carve out features. The body should be slightly smaller than the head. Sand smooth, paint white and then brown. Add features and varnish.

2 For arms, cut hole in centre of fabric. Tack around edge of hole. Roll in short edges of fabric and join with tacking stiches.

3 Make smaller roll for head-dress in same way. Decorate arms and head-dress with gold braid or ribbon. Push balsa wood body through neck hole and secure at back with a tack. Tack the head-dress to the top of the head.

4 Make a long skirt from cotton material (see page 13). Secure skirt to the body with tacks. Sew shoulder straps in place. Edge three sides of the sari with braid. Pin sari to top of head-dress. Drape around the head and under the arms. Tack at front.

5 Add strings: sew one length of string to both 'hands' leaving a loop between. Sew second loop to top of head and middle of back. Decorate with nose jewellery and sequins.

Marionettes

This splendid marionette comes from the very strong tradition of string puppets in Burma. In the eighteenth century, King Bodawpays appointed a Minister for the Theatre. Puppet performances became popular, and many plays were developed. They were a mixture of Hindu and Buddhist traditions. King Bodawpays intended the performances to be educational as well as entertaining.

Performances lasted all night, with one play extending over six or seven nights. Some puppets had as many as fifty or sixty strings, with a moveable mouth and eyes. The plays were performed on a bamboo stage with curtains behind to hide the puppeteers. The puppets were traditionally stored on either side of the stage, the evil characters on the left and the good ones on the right.

This puppet's white face and decorated clothes show him to be a Prince Regent. Two of these princes appear in the plays, one with a white face and the other with a red face. The prince wears trousers and a *dhoti* (loincloth), which is worn by male Hindus.

Make a marionette prince

1 Form a ball of newspaper around cardboard tube and secure with tape. Add features with paper and tape. Cover with layers of papier mâché. When dry, paint face and varnish. Cut circle of card, pierce hole in centre and glue to neck.

You will need: newspaper • cardboard tube • masking tape • papier mâché materials • paints • varnish • card disc • balsa wood for body, two pieces 8 x 13 x 15 cm • glue • eyelet • knitting needle • modelling clay • strong string • thin wire • button • wood: for arms, two pieces 1 x 3 x 7 cm, two pieces 1 x 3 x 10 cm; for legs, two pieces 1 x 3 x 10 cm, two pieces 1 x 3 x 16 cm • coloured fabric • narrow scarf • felt • wood for control: one piece 1 x 3 x 14 cm, two pieces 1 x 3 x 8 cm

2 Glue upper and lower body in T shape. Screw eyelet into neck. Pierce holes through upper and lower body with knitting needle. Make hands and feet from modelling clay. Pierce two small holes in each. Paint and varnish.

3 Pierce hole in head with knitting needle. Make threading needle from thin wire folded in half. Knot string to button, thread through head and tie to eyelet. Grip each wooden limb firmly in vice and drill holes at either end.

arms

legs

4 Tie hands, arms and upper body with string. Do same with feet and legs. Measure from hand to hand and from neck to knees. Cut out a simple fabric jacket with a back piece and two front pieces. Sew and hem edges. Cut collar pieces from felt and glue onto jacket.

5 Sew two fabric tubes for trousers. Tack to legs. For dhoti, wind scarf around waist and between legs.

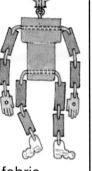

Glue jacket onto puppet. Cut star hat from felt. Glue together. Make a small hole in top of hat.

6 Make string control by nailing a short piece of wood to each end of the long piece. Thread head string through hole in hat and attach to button. Glue hat onto head. Tie other strings to puppet, and tie or loop around control as shown. To operate puppet, hold control in one hand and loops in the other.

Animal string puppets

Animals are always firm favourites in a puppet play. This lovely elephant comes from India. It is made entirely of wood, with a fabric neck to allow its head to move freely. The string controls are very simple. The elephant looks very expressive as it walks across the stage and raises its trunk.

The horse and rider appear in the traditional Kathputli play about the Rajput warrior, Amar Singh Rathore (see page 6). He came to visit the court of the Moghul Emperor Shah Jahan, who built the famous Taj Mahal in northern India.

Make a horse and rider

You will need: newspaper · 3 pipe cleaners or wire · tissue paper · masking tape · fabric for horse, 21 x 30 cm · card · glue · cord for legs, 2 x 40 cm · beads and bells · braid, felt or ribbon trim · ribbon or felt for saddle, 18 x 4 cm · coloured string, 30 cm long · balsa wood, 8 x 1.5 x 1.5 cm · paints · varnish · felt for jacket, 15 x 4 cm · felt for trousers, 8.5 x 7 cm

1 Roll and fold a sheet of tabloid newspaper.

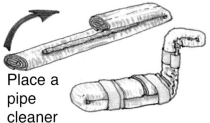

Place a pipe cleaner inside paper and fix with masking tape. Bend to form horse shape. Wrap another piece of folded newspaper and then tissue paper around the body. Fix with tape.

2 Wrap and sew small pieces of fabric around the nose and rear of horse. Wind 3-cm strips of fabric around whole horse. Cut ears from card. Paint and glue in bend of neck.

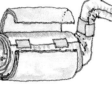

3 Tuck front leg cord under fabric. Stitch back leg cord to middle of horse's back. Thread beads and bells onto legs and knot. Stick braid around body. Attach saddle by stapling or glueing ends together under body.

4 Stitch coloured string to head, saddle and rear, leaving enough for tail. Wrap and glue on braid for bridle. Use beads, felt or fabric paint for eyes.

5 Fix balsa wood in vice. Model rider's head with a craft knife. Paint and varnish. Twist pipe cleaner around body for arms.

6 Cut out simple shape jacket and glue onto rider. Do the same with trousers. Tie braid around jacket. Fix pipe cleaner to hand as a whip. Stick rider to saddle.

Putting on a play

In some areas of the world puppet theatre is very complex, involving a whole group of people to operate the puppets, play the music and narrate the poems and plays. Highly trained people do these jobs, and for them it is a lifetime's work.

However, most forms of puppet theatre are produced very simply in a market-place or a village setting, using very few props and equipment. One puppeteer does everything himself, with great skill.

When you have made a puppet you might want to perform for other people. You can do this very simply, by setting up a stage to suit your needs and preparing a performance.

Before you invite other people to watch, practise by operating your puppet in front of a mirror.

A team effort

Staging a play can involve as many people as you like. You could persuade friends to play the music for you, to handle the lighting, design and print the tickets, look after the audience or make refreshments.

You may wish to put on a more adventurous performance by getting some friends to make other characters and join you. If you are making these puppets as part of a school project, get together with everyone and decide on the best play to perform.

Making stages for your puppets

1 Cut three sides of a television-style square from a large cardboard box. Fold and tape down to form a small stage. Cut a door in the side. Pin backcloths to the inside back of the box.

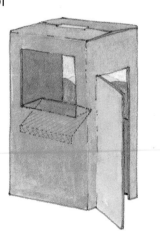

2 Lay a table upside down on the floor. Tape long garden canes to two front legs. Stretch a length of fabric between the canes and another between the back table legs.

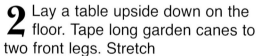
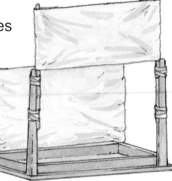

A play idea for all the puppets

An Emperor has a very beautiful daughter. He wants to find a prince for her to marry. As there is no one suitable in any of his neighbours' kingdoms, he sends his horseman out into the world to give notice of a competition. Everyone is invited to come and entertain his court. The best one will marry the Princess.

From far and wide the suitors come. First the Princess and her friends entertain them. Then each one performs something before the court: a song, a proverb, a story, a dance or a fight. The Princess gives each one a different coloured flag to hold.

The Emperor cannot decide upon the winner because they are all so good.

Finally he asks the Princess to decide herself. She says that she has been so excited by their contributions that she has decided to travel the world, seeing for herself all the countries and their peoples. She jumps onto the elephant's back and rides away while everyone waves their flags and sings and dances.

If you want to make this a longer play, you could introduce some trouble. Perhaps an evil sorcerer comes to court and uses his magic powers to kidnap the Princess. Then you will have to decide on a way to defeat the sorcerer and end the play on a happy note.

Glove and rod puppets need a high stage with some form of covering so that the puppeteer cannot be seen (1). String puppets and marionettes should have a low stage so that you can manipulate them from above. In India, string puppet operators often use a sari stretched about one metre above the ground between two poles (2). Shadow puppets require a special screen (3 or 4).

---

3 Using two tables, one upside down on top of the other, stretch a tablecloth across the front at the bottom, and a white sheet across the top. Make sure the sheet is absolutely flat. Fix a small, clip-on reading lamp to back table leg. Operate puppets from behind.

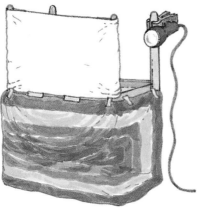

4 Stretch sheet across doorway, fixing it with drawing pins. Stretch thicker piece of fabric across lower part of doorway. Place an anglepoise lamp to one side so that it throws light upwards onto the back of the screen.

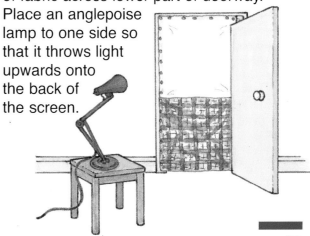

Useful information

United Kingdom

Some helpful addresses

Barnet Multicultural Study Centre
Barnet Teachers' Centre
451 High Road, Finchley
LONDON N12 0AS

Japan Information and
Cultural Centre
101–104 Piccadilly,
LONDON W1V 9FN

Equipment and materials

L. Davenport & Co.
51 Great Russell Street,
LONDON WC1
(swazzles and ventriloquism)

Supreme Magic Co.
64 Berwick Street, LONDON W1
(swazzles and ventriloquism)

Hobby Stores
39 Parkway, LONDON NW1
(balsa wood and craft equipment)

The Puppet Centre
Battersea Arts Centre
Lavender Hill, LONDON SW11

The Rhythm Box
5 Denmark Street, LONDON WC2
(noise makers, bird pipes, sirens etc.)

UNIMA (Union Internationale de la
Marionnette)
Percy Press II,
16 Templeton Road,
LONDON N15

Museums

Bethnal Green Museum of
Childhood
Cambridge Heath Road
LONDON E2

Derby Museum and Art Gallery
The Strand, DERBY

Edinburgh Museum of Childhood
34 High Street, EDINBURGH

Horniman Museum and Library
London Road, Forest Hill
LONDON SE23

Merseyside County Museums
William Brown Street
LIVERPOOL

The Museum of Mankind
6 Burlington Gardens
Piccadilly, LONDON W1

National Toy Museum
Rottingdean Grange
Rottingdean, BRIGHTON

Pitt Rivers Museum
University of Oxford
Parks Road, OXFORD

Polka Children's Theatre
240 The Broadway
Wimbledon, LONDON SW19

Pollock's Toy Museum
1 Scala Street, LONDON W1

Sunderland Music Hall Museum
Gordon Place, SUNDERLAND

The Theatre Museum
Covent Garden, LONDON WC1

Puppets for sale

Bangladesh Centre of
East London
185a Cannon Street Road
LONDON E1 2LX

Centaur Gallery
82 Highgate High Street
LONDON N6
(antique puppets)

Jackson Contra-Banned
Unit 2, Gatehouse Enterprise
Centre, Albert Street, Lockwood
HUDDERSFIELD HD1 3QD
(artefacts from Indonesia, Peru,
Columbia, China, Thailand,
Philippines and Jamaica – mail
order catalogue, education packs)

Joliba
47 Colston Street
BRISTOL BS1 5AX
(arts from Mali and the Niger Bend
– mail order catalogue and
education supplement)

Soma Books Ltd
38 Kennington Lane
LONDON SE11 4LS
(Indian craft list)

Books

The Complete Book of Puppet
Theatre
David Currell (A. & C. Black)

Fresh Start: Puppets
Lyndie Wright (Watts Books)

Fresh Start: Toy Theatres
Lyndie Wright (Watts Books)

The KnowHow Book of Puppets
Violet Philpott & M.J.McNeil
(Usborne)

Of Muppets and Men
Christopher Finch (Michael
Joseph)

Rainy Days: Puppets and
Shadow Theatre
Denny Robson (Watts Books)

The World of Puppets
Rene Simmen (Elsevier–Phaidon)

Australia

Museums

Australian Toy Museum
1st Floor, 180 Smith Street
Collingwood Victoria 3066
phone: 03 419 4138

Sydney Children's Museum Inc
crn Pitt and Walpole Streets
Merrylands NSW
phone: 02 897 1414

Museum of Childhood
Edith Cowan University
Claremont Western Australia
phone: 09 442 1373

Puppets for sale

Murray Raine Puppets
22 Silver Street
Marrickville NSW
phone: 02 550 0198

Glossary

ancestors Past members of a family.

backcloth A painted scene hung at the back of a stage.

balsa Very soft, light wood from the balsa tree.

Buddha The title given to the founder of the Buddhist faith. It means 'the enlightened one'.

characteristics Distinctive marks of a person's character.

dhoti A cloth garment worn round the waist and between the legs.

emigrant Someone who goes to live in another country.

fable A short story that is not based on fact. Sometimes it teaches a moral lesson.

gamelan **orchestra** An Indonesian instrumental group who play for religious ceremonies and dramas.

incarnation The appearance, in human form, often of a god or a devil.

kimono A long, loose Japanese robe.

marionette A puppet operated from above by strings.

Moghul The Mongolian word for a great or important person.

moral tale A story that is intended to teach good behaviour.

Prince Regent A prince who acts on behalf of a young king.

props Objects used as part of a play or performance.

proverb A wise saying.

ric rac braid A decorative fabric border that is made in a 'wave' shape.

ruff A starched frill worn round the neck in some European countries during the sixteenth century.

sari A length of fabric draped around the body. It is worn by Hindu women.

scimitar A crescent-shaped sword carried by Moslem soldiers.

scoring A fold line that is made by denting a piece of paper or card with a blunt object.

sorcerer A person who makes evil magic.

suitor A man who wishes to marry a certain woman.

supernatural being A spirit or being that cannot be seen in the natural world.

Taj Mahal A tomb in India which was built by the Moghul Emperor Shah Jahan to honour his dead wife.

transparent Able to be seen through.

zanni Traditional clowns in the Italian *commedia dell'arte* theatre.

Index

Additional photographs:

page 10, C. Bowman/Robert Harding Picture Library; page 20, Japan National Tourist Office, London.